Being a Princess is *so* Yesterday

Melissa Hunt

E.A.H Publishing—Assonet, MA
ISBN: 978-0-578-79541-6
Library of Congress Control Number: 2020921923
Title:*Being a Princess is so Yesterday*
Author: Melissa Hunt
Digital distribution | 2020
Paperback | 2020

Dedication

This book is dedicated to my wonderful and amazing daughter, Elizabeth. Never let anyone tell you, you can't do something.

You can achieve all of your goals and dreams.

Being a princess is so yesterday, there are so many other great things I could be.

I could be an airplane pilot, flying around the world or
I could be an architect and design the tallest tower.

4

Maybe when I grow up, I will be a doctor caring for others or a veterinarian helping animals.

I could be a firefighter putting out fires
or an electrician connecting all of the wires.

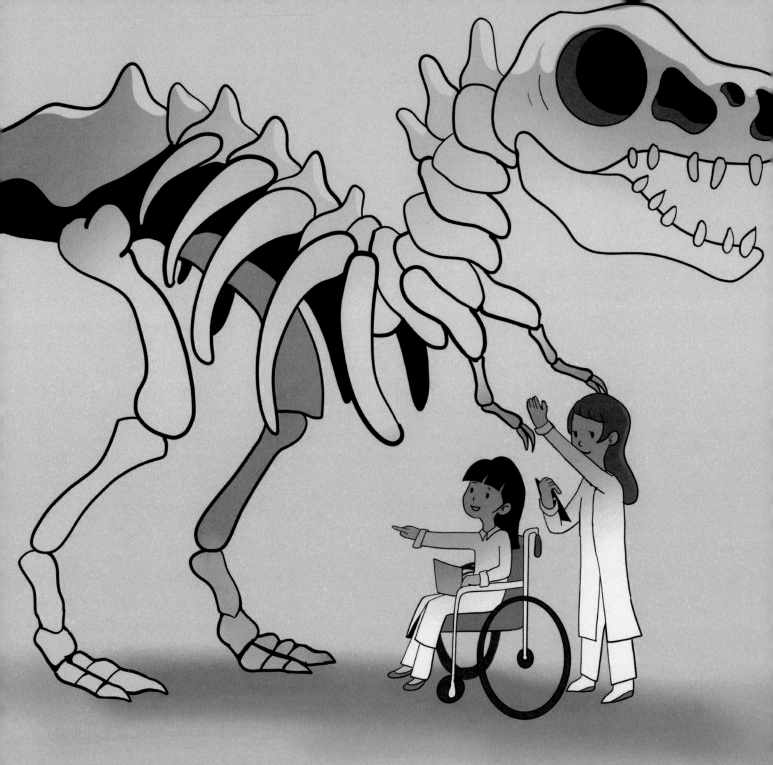

I think when I grow up, I could be a Paleontologists studying dinosaurs.

Or an out of this world Astronaut, exploring the universe.

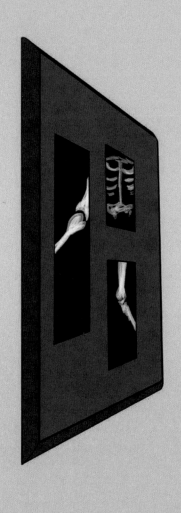
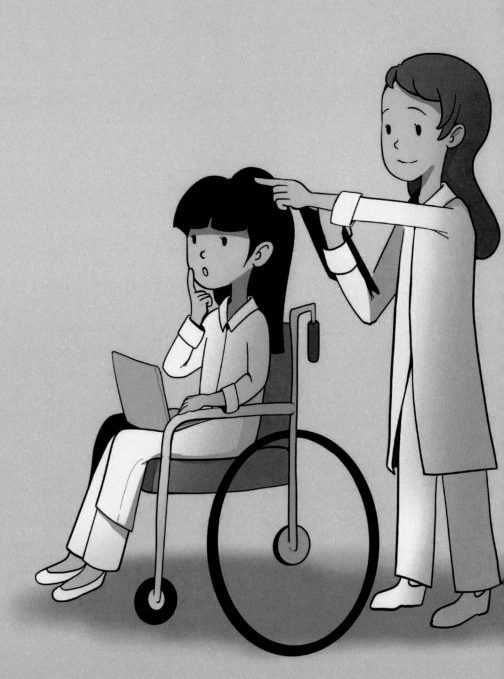

I could be a Radiologist looking at X-rays

Or be a Marine Biologist studying sting rays.

I could be a Football player, kicking the ball between the goal
post
Or a Referee making sure the rules of the game are followed.

I could grow up to be a Scientist, making important discoveries
Or I could even be the President making important decisions.

No matter what I will be when I grow up, I am going to be amazing.

Made in the USA
Middletown, DE
23 November 2020